Exhumation

Sean Eason

BookLeaf
Publishing

India | USA | UK

Presentation by *BookLeaf Publishing*

Web: www.bookleafpub.com

E-mail: info@bookleafpub.com

ISBN: 9789363306301

First edition 2024

Urban Planning

It was a generous winter, abundant in icy glaze
and winds that caught our chests like a sail.
I would pause in open doorways or over sewer
grates,
just to catch a hint of warm air.

I rode buses often, and, on one route,
I saw an older man with a fierce geometry.
He sat across the aisle, a trickle of passengers
between us.
He caught my eye, flashed two rows of
egg-white teeth.

I thought of snow-capped mountains, segmented
sidewalks,
saw Pompeii's cobbled streets reaching for the
sea
as Vesuvius heaved up a cloud of ash—and fled,
my mouth filling with saliva and the taste of
cigarettes.

For years, I avoided front gates and entrance
halls,
preferring the raised wax-edge
where a warm knife can find purchase—

till I found a magpie's nest, discarded by some
indifferent tree.
Among these trinkets—clumps of cotton, shards
of sea glass,
and shirt buttons—was a creased, sepia-toned
photograph
from some forgotten family album:

A tall man in silhouette, standing between rows
of graves.
In the distance, tombs and skyscrapers.
The cemetery became a city—the city, a
cemetery.

Origin of Darwin

He never fit his spine like his father,
a corpulent, ever-expanding man
who dressed it tall.

Death stripped it, gave it weight,
left the bones to grow in the youngest son,
who did not have the shoulders for it.

He surrendered in the end, developing
a stoop that rendered a six-foot frame
crooked and small.

Of his mother, he remembered only
a black velvet gown. He saw it at funerals,
on mannequins. When he sat on the banks
of rivers watching his float ripple the surface—
he saw the gown carried by the current
between thin shadows on the far shore.
He saw it in endless forms, till it stretched
thinner

and thinner. He saw it for the last time
on an afternoon in the woods near Cambridge,
where he collected a single egg
from each bird's nest, a few plants,

and, under the peeling bark of an aged tree,
two beetles with a carapace shaped just so,
a thorax fused there instead of here.

Admiring them, one in each hand, he caught
a shimmer of black from extended wings,
taking flight.

Crow Tries the Truth

"Were I the Moor," Crow began.
He faltered; it was doubt
in his part, in his speech.

"I could be no less," Crow said.
Again, in his speech, he knew—
this was somewhat less than true.

He held sleep like a memory,
but the dew formed, gave faces
to the lonely Crow.

To each, rapt and reflected,
Crow could be naught but honest.
"I am not a benevolent God."

But they were set, spoon-fed
with shovels for their demons
and empty glasses for their dreams.

In light of their doubt,
Crow became a roiling sea
to teach them of his cruelty.

The faces learned, became

what they beheld—
a storm, swirling round

the lonely Crow—the eye.
Crow was like an Albatross,
and the Albatross a Crow.

Neither could suffer
the other to be,
and so they burnt

in Blue and Green—
a boiling sea.
Dew flashed, like sparks

and died as such.
In stillness, settled,
unmade—Crow was no more.

Chronicle of the Monster

Part I; Discovery

We are nature, like music
from under the Earth.
I've been indeterminate—
spent the past year as a ghost.

I dreamt I was a word—
like comedy or tragedy—
found dragons in men
and men in clouds.

I pulled a pebble from your eye
and watched you crumble—
followed the path of rock
that fell and found

a monster worse than I
standing midst the circled stones.
A reflection of
the way we touched the Earth;

fingers piercing ground,
beast in the palm
of the sunken hand
which grasps—then gives.

Chronicle of the Monster

Part II; Hypocrisy

Metronome-mouth
with your tongue-tick beat—
I've seen the monster in you.

You pluck words, like strings,
from a well-oiled throat,
eulogize like glowing coals

that blink themselves to death—
or the cicada chorus
that sounds itself to silence.

You remind me of
my mother's cabinets;
full of good China,

silver and glass—
beneath which, I saw
water swollen wood,

weak and rotten.
Mother never did forgive me
for speaking of it.

Chronicle of the Monster

Part III; Prophecy

I imagine you, risen
from the grave in flame and fury—
a gross mockery of birth,
delivered unto scorched Earth.
Clawed and crawling, worm-like,
festering flesh and fetid breath.

Do I become what I behold?
An ever expanding hollow,
fragmented, carapaced.
Non-existence could not dissuade me.
Nor the void. What threat, the abyss,
to a monster who seeks the grave?

Golemancy

When the alchemist left his tower
        in hunt of herbs and metal,
his sentinel—ever silent—stood
        and, dutiful, waited—
and would wait, midst lichen and brick,
        for centuries, still.

When the woods around had their fill
        of the "still" and the "wait,"
they sought to slake other hungers.
        And so, with root and vine,
crept in and up and over—
        crawled, consuming.

When stone stood or fell only
        by sylvan hand,
when windows, framed in ivy, shed glass
        for branch and leaf,
when the floor forgot footsteps
        in favor of flowers—

then the sentinel, stone hearted,
        more patient, even,
than the forest for its trees
        in brief victory—

then, odd and ancient, awful relic
        long forgotten; then he woke.

Epitaph

"Crow
Grinned
Crying: 'This is my creation,'
Flying the black flag of himself."
-Crow Blacker Than Ever, by Ted Hughes

Life is bound to the dirt.
I'd rather be scattered, ash
upon the winds and waves,
breathed and born by tongues.

Scattered, like dregs of tea
in the depths of mugs—
divining meaning from
the geometry of gore.

Like broken shards of pottery
collecting the morning dew—
a purpose remembered
by the forgotten whole.

Scattered—the smell of cigarettes.
I lingered outside my apartment
in a cloud of smoke, breathing in ash
and letting it lie upon my tongue.

An impatient Crow,
hopping from foot to foot,
wanted words to define it,
but could only croak and caw.

Scattered, even Crow's cries—
eclipsed by the chorus
of the feathered flock,
which rose; a black, beleaguered sun.

Nightmare Fragments

I.

i limbless writhe hiding still
his pendulum eyes seeking
sweep the brush over me
i swear each pass pause and
i cannot breathe for fear
his eyes will linger longer still

II.

Like a corpse forgotten upon a distant shore—
sallow, bloated—the Lake House sleeps, silent,
waiting for the waves of dream to drag me there.

And in that house resides a haunting, gentle
thing.
It roams the halls—which creak like brittle
bones,
low and soft—holding secrets in there quiet
keep.

For fear of this, my lungs swell—pregnant
with a terror I cannot name. Away—
to the lake, a mirror, dark and deep:

In it's depths I hope to find
a quiet place,
a quiet mind.

Moulting

He says, "the seats in the back
go down," then he fucks
me on the floor
of his sister's SUV.
Only an hour before,
we were mumble-singing, shy
and drunk at a small patio table
behind some bar
under a bruise-purple sky.

I walk home
alone, shed
another skin.
So many husks
now, in my wake.
And me; skin raw
and clean—new.

De Historia Piscium

In 1992, Washington state was puddles and
pavement.
A local joke claimed the Kitsap would soon sink
into the Sound.

Born in Bremerton that May—
where civilization was
like river silt on the bank—
my definition of silence was set
by a steady metronome of rain
ticking at eighty BPM.
Dry existed only in advertisements—
tan families vacationing at the beach
or the Grand Canyon.

At four, I flew from the sea-blue,
sea-green coast to sun-soaked Florida.
The horizon was all wrong. I hid
from company in kitchens, where
I learned to crimp and flute crust.
My speech was as clipped as the wings
of my mother's birds. I memorized
geography and "The Raven,"
but forgot birthdays and faces.

This year, I walked out into a storm
and every raindrop missed me.

18

Omphaloskepsis

"He loves me." Crow plucked one of his
feathers.
"He loves me not." Crow plucked another.
Each fell: the first became a crack—
the second, pavement around it.

"He loves me—He loves me not." Two more
fell,
together. They became an island.
But the crack, displeased, swallowed this.
Crow would not see the destruction;

his pace only quickened. The sky became
a storm of feathers—the world all puddles.
Crow felt as common as a Rooster,
continued to fret until
Crow had no feathers left.
And what is a crow
without feathers?

You Fit Into Me

20

Like water into water—
Hereafter, inseparable—
Indistinct.

One becomes the other.
One disappears.
Both.

Surface Tension

Silver flash—like the eye flicker,
the panicked flutter of wings
before the fall. There—

the ink-injecting needle, relentless and exact,
plunges into the skin—
pierced and pierced again.

Of course it hurt,
as all things should;
just enough to matter.

He was warned this would be permanent—
met prophecy with a laugh.
"No more than I."

Anxiety

Jumbled words, phrases; clipped, half-formed.
What I mean to say has no voice.

I see egg shells in the sky.
I worry we're all more delicate
than we look. I worry about gravity.

With my hand on your thigh, I fear
I may worry a hole in your jeans
the way my thumb traces its regular track—
there and back, there and back…

But if I stop, I know: my too-still tongue—
sitting stagnant, rusted—
will offend.

The world has not ended, but skips
like a record. Maybe it's me.

A body—surface tension;
rippled, but unbroken.

A Mirror

You belong in the fields, where
planted pikes threaten violence
against the sky.

When last you stood that line,
you curled in—like a burnt match
or dead centipede.

How dry was the air; you thought
of expensive red wines and
the crunch of dead leaves.

What a sickly flame; afraid
to burn and afraid to stop—
you flicker weakly.

You should move with elegance;
treat every step like a dance,
choreographed.

But you travel vague patterns,
 constructing forests of knots,
labyrinthian.

Simple Canon

We breathe. We move. It seems so simple,
but what's simple is never easy.
See how we flow from form
to form? This dance is balance—
Feel the beat; be light, but rough.
We serve like puppets, pulled by strings.

We stand, all still and straight. All alike, alone.
But more together than we've ever known.
Our arms and legs in sync, as one. Begin.
We step away and towards each other. Again.
Always in cycles. We end where we began,
though
It's never quite the same. Now, lead. I'll follow.

Arabesque

25

A master weave may seem in flawless form;
so solid—smooth—cut straight from the fabric
of the world. A likeness born
of needle and thread.

I think I prefer this quick,
amateur craft of a crude scarf.
Wool, black and thick
in a loose and clumsy stitch,
which held to light
would seem a starry night.

Better still, a spider's web,
the act—before it was art.
How minimal, these thin
silken strands, invisible—
but for the glance of day,
whose eye cast it ablaze.

It's the difference seen between
the gear and the heart,
the typewriter and the brush.

Summer Storms

The summer day fills with an anxious,
insect-like hum. A mother and her youngest son
are inside. He peels apples, leaving long,
spiraling trails of red skin. They chat
without consequence. Outside, the granddaughter
is all eyes and pointing. Her grandfather
stands next to a grill and a plate of steaks,
arms crossed and eyes on the river.

The tide quickens, the air swells with wind,
the sun disappears behind ripening clouds.
A box of fireworks grows sodden
as the family flees indoors.

Worried about the middle son,
unreachable on some now slick stretch
of interstate, the mother thinks to call
his—don't say boyfriend—roommate.
The granddaughter presses her face
against the sliding-glass door.

Weaveworld

I. "Book Three: Out of the Empty Quarter"

I learned Liverpool was a storm: dark and
dignified—
the victorian attempt at Venice. It was all bridges
and coast—which was visible from every
window,
not more than two streets off. There were no
clouds
to mar the sky, but flocks of birds could blot out
the sun.
The streets were all cobbled, and the houses
could boast
of the generations they'd born. It contained its
own cities
and its own self-concept. "Always, worlds
within worlds."

II. "Book Two: The Fugue"

He rose—grinning, like some freakish sun from
a children's show—
hooking a finger over the novel's spine to pull it
down.

The words on the page—"Can you name
one?"—were replaced
by a freckle on the tendon of his neck, leading
down
to the clavicle and the scattered constellation of
freckles
and scars beyond. "There are worse things than
existence—"
the ink of the words had seeped into my finger
tips, and I feared
my touch would convey the Hag's response:
"Can you name one?"

III. "Book One: In the Kingdom of the Cuckoo"

Before I began, I pressed a slip of potato skin
between two pages, leaving a stain of starch
and a fertile stench. The first page declared,
"Nothing ever begins," and smelled like a
garden—
not like the flowers, but the dirt in which they
grew.
The mixing bowl's motor began to hum from the
kitchen,
reducing a dozen peeled potatoes to a damp,
delicious mush.
Book one, part one, chapter one, section one:
"Nothing ever begins."

Another Earth

I should describe the manicured lawn;
the it's-a-boy-blue sky; the lacquered coffin
adorned with wreaths; the mourners
arranged around the grave. The departed rested
on an easel—with a frozen, yearbook-photo
grin.
The priest's eulogy droned on as ants formed
a rough seam along the edge of the coffin lid.

Instead, I fled the service to wander St.
Augustine,
where I felt a quiet immortality in the stones.
Parades had marched across the Bridge of Lions,
under the gaze of its eponymous marble
guardians,

and the surface of the Matanzas mocked them
all,
reflecting a silent, watery march—indifferent.
Fireworks ran across the night's dome,
blooming in brief color.

History haunted the city, thickening the air.
Places with long memory bred ghosts.